Half of Nowhere

Riddles and Spells

Richard Burns

Illustrated by Nick Maland

 CAMBRIDGE UNIVERSITY PRESS

Cambridge Reading

General Editors
Richard Brown and Kate Ruttle

Consultant Editor
Jean Glasberg

For Arijana

PUBLISHED BY THE PRESS SYNDICATE OF THE UNIVERSITY OF CAMBRIDGE
The Pitt Building, Trumpington Street, Cambridge CB2 1RP, United Kingdom

CAMBRIDGE UNIVERSITY PRESS
The Edinburgh Building, Cambridge CB2 2RU, United Kingdom
40 West 20th Street, New York, NY 10011-4211, USA
10 Stamford Road, Oakleigh, Melbourne 3166, Australia

Text © Richard Burns 1998
Illustrations © Nick Maland 1998

First published 1998

Printed in the United Kingdom at the University Press, Cambridge

Typeset in Concorde

A catalogue record for this book is available from the British Library

ISBN 0 521 47626 7 paperback

CONTENTS

On the heath, in the park,
I can soar like a lark.

I can dance, leap and twirl,
I can prance, plunge and swirl.

With the wind in my tail,
Cloud-high I sail.

I've no toes but one foot,
And no mouth but one head,
I've no body but four legs,
In your room, with fine sheets spread.

4

I take two steps forward. The battle's begun.
Then I go slow. I can only take one.
No matter whether white or black
I pounce at an angle when I attack.
I may be tiny but I'm tough and mean
To end up wearing the crown of queen.

*A*t my start
I'm lots of bits.
At my end
Each bit fits.

*I*f the night were a Christmas tree,
We'd be the spangles and orbs you see
Adorning it, turned off, turned on,
But by the dawn, completely gone.

*A*ren't I clever? Well, could you speak,
If instead of your mouth, you had my beak?

*I*f this old man were Everest,
I'd be the snow that topped his crest.

I'm found in a zoo but am more of a **zee**,
Not a **chump** or a **champ**
But a scallywag scamp
And you won't find a naughtier **imp** than me.

*B*low . . .
I'll grow.
Stop!
I'll pop.

*M*y first part's a colouring for hair,
My second is half of nowhere.
My third, the opposite of dive,
My whole, you'll never find alive.

I never bite or bark or growl,
Nor do I wag my tail or howl.
Quite tame, I wouldn't hurt a soul,
Warm and snug inside my roll.
Most kids like me best, of course,
Blanketed in tomato sauce.

*T*o use me, point me and take aim,
I'll shoot you, but won't kill or maim.
I'll capture you with flash and click
But never touch you. My best trick
Is triggering your memory
Of who you were, while you go free.

I break into foam
On the shore as I die,
And I am your hand
Dancing goodbye!

*B*y the sea, my first half builds castles high,
And my second rides a broom through the sky.

I'm partly **rust**,
And yet you must
Rely on me till the world's end
If you would keep a true friend.

10

*H*ey diddle diddle,
I'll ask you a riddle.
What has a head and a tail
But no middle?

I'm the space enclosed by the uniform bend
Of one line without beginning or end.

*T*ake anything from itself to find
I'm the empty hole it leaves behind.

Is that a blush or rust on your chest,
Cheeky chirper – and where is your nest?

Long ears bob upon the heath.
We sleep in burrows underneath.

By the bank of the river,
When a breeze whispers, Why?
See my green hair quiver:
Can a tree cry?

12

I sit on a sea of hair,
On curls I seem to sail,
I can cover the top of a pony tail
Or shade a bald patch from the glare.

We won't cut you, though we do have blades,
And you'll find us in gardens and deep wooded glades.
We'd rather be short as a surface for sport
Like tennis at Wimbledon or cricket at Lords.

Red flying tots
With black spots.

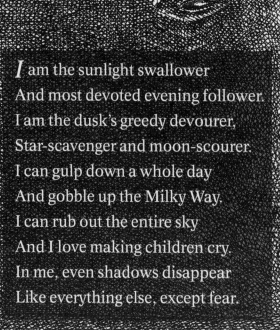

I am the sunlight swallower
And most devoted evening follower.
I am the dusk's greedy devourer,
Star-scavenger and moon-scourer.
I can gulp down a whole day
And gobble up the Milky Way.
I can rub out the entire sky
And I love making children cry.
In me, even shadows disappear
Like everything else, except fear.

*P*rod me. You can't dent me.
Sea, rain and river sent me.
I nourish you and swathe you,
Wash, refresh and bathe you,
But I can maim and scathe you.
If you're a fire, I'll quench you.
Stand under me, I'll drench you.

I picture you twice as far
From myself as you really are.

15

We're well armoured but we're not tanks,
We move in lines and rows and ranks.
Good soldiers and diligent workers,
In our society there are no shirkers.
We live in a nest but we're not birds,
We're not cattle but we throng in herds.
We're well organised, efficient, clean,
Loyal servants to our royal queen.

Open, I'll shield you from hail, sleet or rain.
Closed, I'm a sword or a stick again.

I'm the millionaire
Of the air.
Tigery flier
Gathering from flower
A millionfold
Richer gold
Than human wealth,
For mine brings health.

16

Showers,
Flowers,
Bud, fresh blood.

Long days,
Bright rays
Of sunlight, short night.

Trees burning,
Cold returning,
Build the fire, higher.

No leaf lingers,
Trees' bony fingers
Spread, as if dead.

*F*our chambered cave
On a red river,
From womb to grave
Your life giver.

*T*he baize on top of a billiard table,
Jungles and forests of truth and fable,
Moss, grassy lawns, leaves, bottle-glass
And emeralds are in my class.

I work all hours and get no pay.
My hands never stop, night or day.

*A*fter the blue spark in the dark
And the yellow flash of the flame,
The fire's gone out, not much is left.
What am I? Can you say my name?

*I*dentical twins, me and my brother,
But the mirror image of each other,
Off we go, I'm left, he's right.
Laced or buckled, we clasp you tight.

19

I rumble and mumble and sometimes I crack
My whip across the whole sky's back.

*W*altzing pincers, waving claws,
I sidestep on the sea's dance floors.

20

*S*ky fluff,
High enough?

I'm made of criss-crosses
And thousands of holes,
And though the sea tosses
I catch shoals and shoals.

*M*y emptiness is so cunningly wound
Upon itself, you can hear the sound
Of waves' distant crash or roar
On the shore.

21

Far thicker beneath bright sunlight
Than under a sky with no moon,
I'm a giant in the evening
But a mere dwarf at noon.
I lie down next to you when it's day
But in pitch darkness I vanish away.

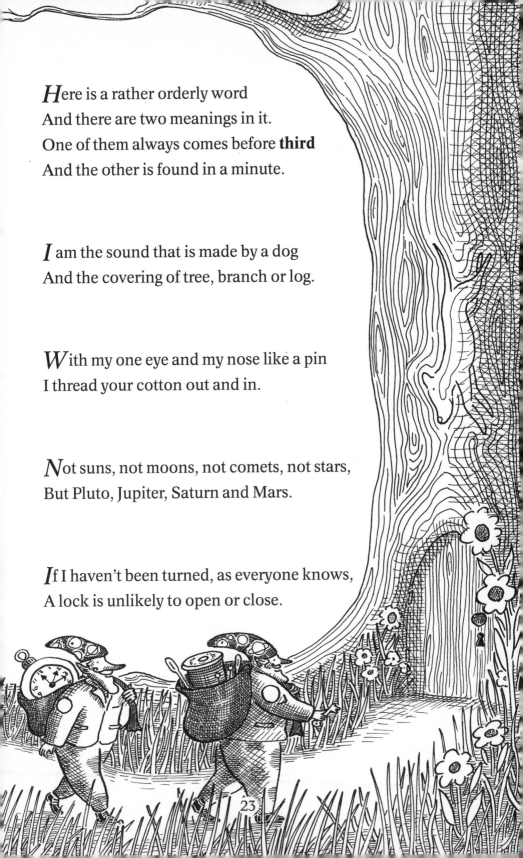

Here is a rather orderly word
And there are two meanings in it.
One of them always comes before **third**
And the other is found in a minute.

I am the sound that is made by a dog
And the covering of tree, branch or log.

With my one eye and my nose like a pin
I thread your cotton out and in.

Not suns, not moons, not comets, not stars,
But Pluto, Jupiter, Saturn and Mars.

If I haven't been turned, as everyone knows,
A lock is unlikely to open or close.

23

*T*oo whit too whoo, twitter hoot howl,
Old feathery round eyes, I'm the wise —— .

*A*braca flipper, abraca flea
I'm a quick nipper, you can't catch —— .

*G*argle with giggle gaggle juice
And you'll lay an egg that'll hatch out a —— .

*T*wist all your fingers and twiddle your toes,
Tell a lie a day, see how your nose —— .

*T*widdle de diddle, twiddle de do,
This is a spell to lace up my —— .

Sour milk, mouldy cheese, burnt toast,
This spell will turn you into a —— .

Swagman, billabong, kulabar koo,
I'll turn you into a —— .

Lullaby billy bee lolly blue peep,
This is a spell to help you to —— .

Titchy, scratchy, witchy, bewitchy,
This is a powder to make you feel —— .

Purr, miaow, stroke me, smooth as silk,
Give me a saucer full of —— .

Wag, woof, dribble, pant and bark,
All I want is a romp in the —— .

A tishy wishy squishy wheeze
This is a spell to make you —— .

Spawn mixed with tadpoles in pond water grog,
This potion will turn a prince to a —— .

Wristy, fisty, shoo and cuff,
Leave me alone, I've had —— .

Fumble, scramble, stay very cool,
Please don't let me be late for —— .

When you're sad or moody or just in a muddle,
This spell will bring you a soft bear to —— .

Come trout, come tiddler, come salmon, come bream,
Please nibble the bait that I've dipped in your —— .

This spell only half-exists in my head.
It hasn't been thought, so it cannot be s—— .
And it hasn't been written, so it cannot be r—— .

*W*as I here or was I not?
These words of mine are all you've got.
Perhaps some spark from them, a seed,
May pass into you as you read.
If you do, you will inherit
Something through them of my spirit.
I lived through words, away they flew,
But through them, hope to live in you.
So am I here or am I not?

ANSWER KEY

Pages 4–5

On the heath
Kite

I've no toes
Bed

I take two steps forward
Pawn (in a game of chess)

At my start
Jigsaw puzzle

Pages 6–7

If the night were
a Christmas tree
Stars

Aren't I clever?
Parrot

If this old man were Everest
White hair

Pages 8–9

I'm found in a zoo
Chimpanzee

Blow . . .
Balloon

My first part's
Dinosaur (Dye – no – soar)

I never bite or bark
Hot dog

To use me, point me
Camera

Pages 10–11

I break into foam
Wave

By the sea, my first
Sandwich (sand + witch)

I'm partly rust
Trust

Hey diddle diddle
Coin

I'm the space enclosed
Circle

Take anything from itself
Zero/nought/nothing

Pages 12–13

Is that a blush or rust
Robin

Long ears bob
Rabbits

By the bank of the river
Weeping willow tree

I sit on a sea of hair
Hat/cap

We won't cut you
Grass

Red flying tots
Ladybirds

Pages 14–15

I am the sunlight swallower
Darkness/night

Prod me. You can't dent me.
Water

I picture you twice as far
Mirror

Pages 16–17

We're well armoured
Ants

Open, I'll shield you
Umbrella

I'm the millionaire
Bee

Showers
The four seasons (spring, summer, autumn, winter)

Pages 18–19
Four chambered cave
Heart

The baize on top of
a billiard table
Green

I work all hours
Clock/watch

After the blue spark
Ash

Identical twins
Shoes

Pages 20–21

I rumble and mumble
Thunderstorm

Waltzing pincers
Crab

Sky fluff
Cloud

I'm made of criss-crosses
Fishing net

My emptiness is so
cunningly wound
Seashell

Pages 22–23

Far thicker beneath
bright sunlight
Shadow

Here is a rather orderly
word
Second

I am the sound
Bark

With my one eye
Needle

Not suns, not moons
Planets

If I haven't been turned
Key

Pages 24–25

Too whit too whoo
Owl

Abraca flipper
Me

Gargle with giggle gaggle
juice
Goose

Twist all your fingers
Grows

Twiddle de diddle
Shoe

Pages 26–27

Sour milk, mouldy cheese
Ghost

Swagman, billabong
Kangaroo

Lullaby billy bee
Sleep

Titchy, scratchy
Itchy

Purr, miaow
Milk

Wag, woof, dribble
Park

A tishy wishy
squishy wheeze
Sneeze

Spawn mixed with
tadpoles
Frog

Wristy, fisty
Enough

Page 28

Fumble, scramble
School

When you're sad or moody
Cuddle

Come trout, come tiddler
Stream

This spell only half-exists
Said
Read

Page 29

Was I here or was I not?
The author of this book